Musical Snapshots

9 Original Solos for the Intermediate Pianist
Portraying Musical Visits Around the World

Martha Mier

Foreword

We often bring a souvenir home with us when we visit a different place. Visits to other countries can be fondly remembered by a souvenir of music. *Musical Snapshots,* Book 2, will guide the intermediate piano student on a musical tour of Japan, Egypt, Hawaii, France, Scotland, Spain, and the United States.

Imagine the mysterious wonder of "Egyptian Pyramids," or the delicate beauty of "Cherry Blossoms in Osaka." The exotic Spanish scene is explored in "Gypsy Guitars" and "Spanish Romance."

I hope you will enjoy a memorable journey to various countries as you play these nine solos in *Musical Snapshots,* Book 2.

Martha Mier

Contents

Alfred Music Publishing Co., Inc.
P.O. Box 10003
Van Nuys, CA 91410-0003
alfred.com

ISBN-10: 0-7390-7767-8
ISBN-13: 978-0-7390-7767-2

Cover Photos:
© istockphoto/(dancer) kparis, (gypsy guitar) emeraldchik, (bagpipes) doughtfulneddy •
© stockxchange/(cherry trees) stararia, (piano) emailrober, (fan) picaland • © PhotoDisc (Hawaii, Paris)

Cherry Blossoms in Osaka

Martha Mier

Egyptian Pyramids

Martha Mier

Moderately

Hawaiian Getaway

Martha Mier

Parisian Waltz

Fast, happily

Martha Mier

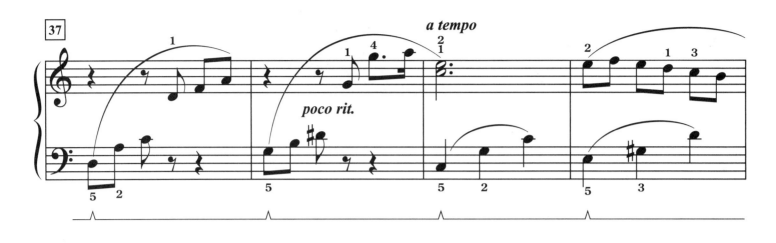

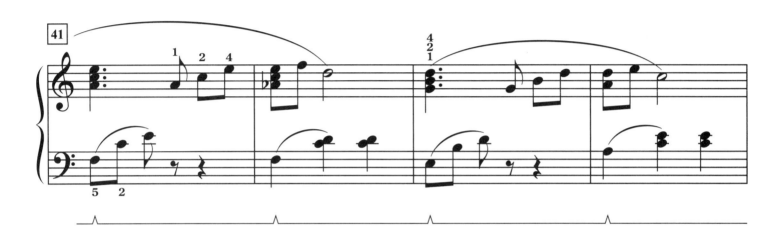

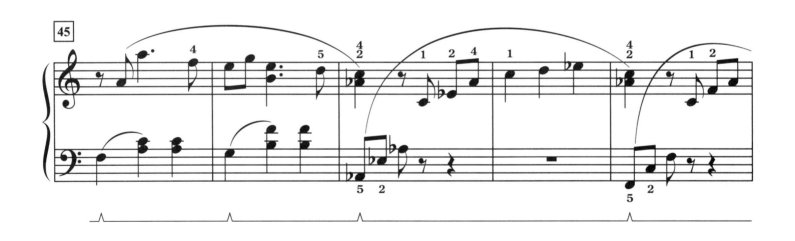

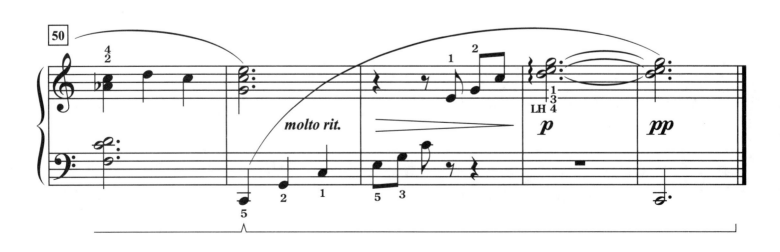

for Jacob Robert Baggett

A Scottish Jig for Jake

Martha Mier

Steadily

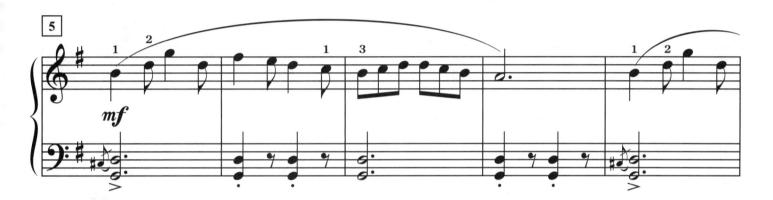

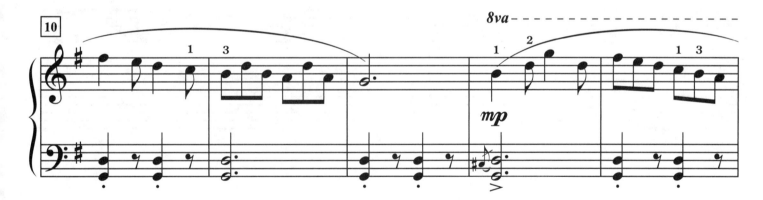

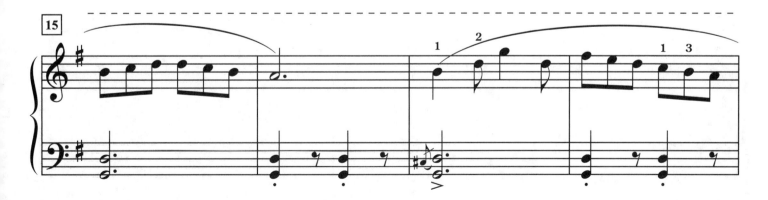

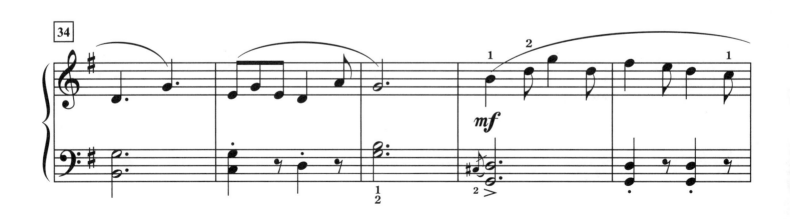

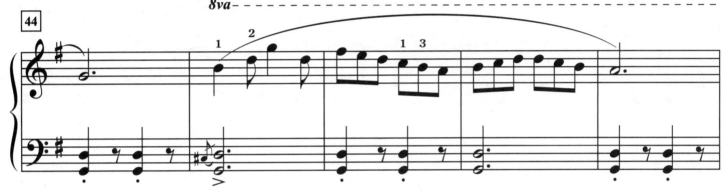

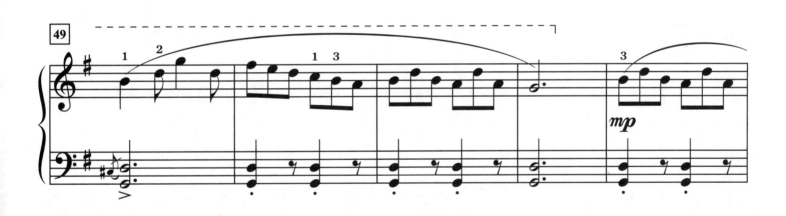

American Ragtime

Martha Mier

Happily

Spanish Suite

I. Gypsy Guitars

Martha Mier

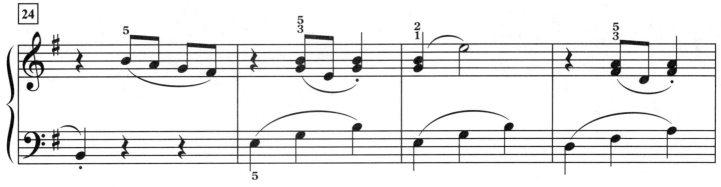

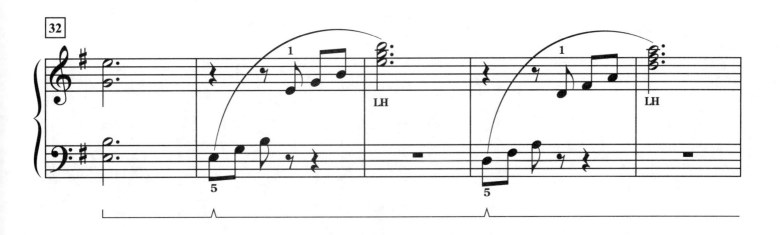

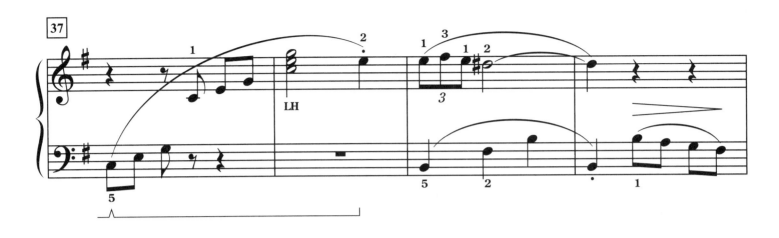

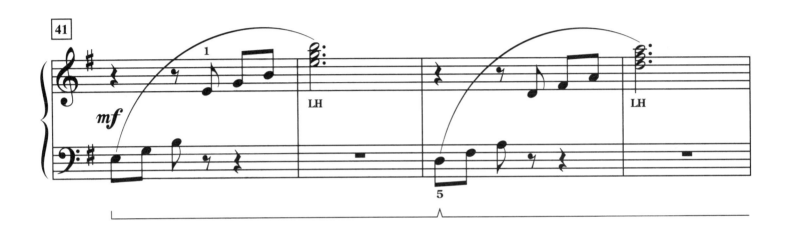

II. Spanish Romance

Martha Mier

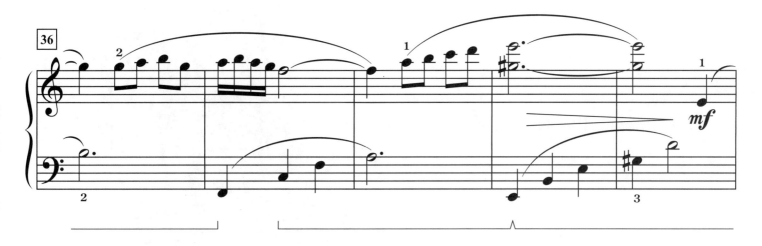

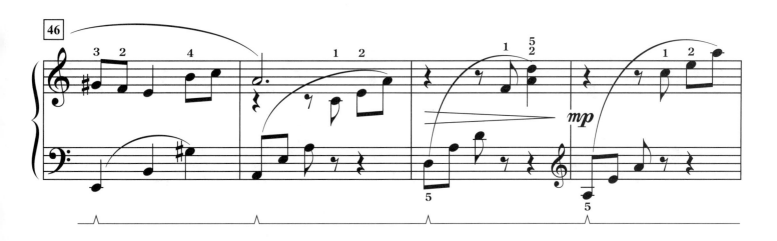

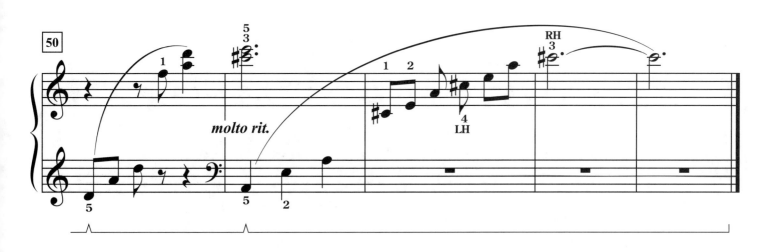

III. Flamenco Dancers

Bold and flashy

Martha Mier

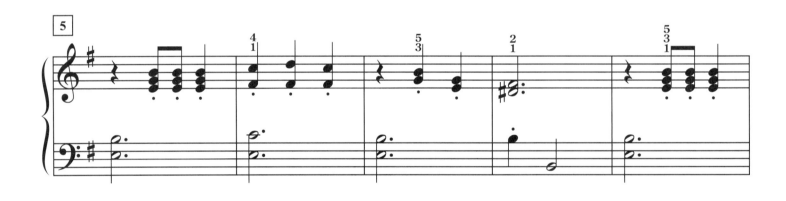

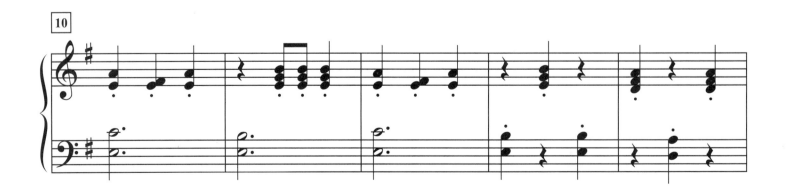